# LEHMAN MARINE DIESEL ENGINE 4D242, 4D254, 6D363, 6D363TC, 6D380

**LEHMAN MARINE DIESEL ENGINE 4D242, 4D254, 6D363, 6D363TC, 6D380**

ISBN/EAN: 9783954272389
Erscheinungsjahr: 2012
Erscheinungsort: Bremen, Deutschland

© maritimepress in Europäischer Hochschulverlag GmbH & Co. KG, Fahrenheitstr. 1, 28359 Bremen. Alle Rechte beim Verlag und bei den jeweiligen Lizenzgebern.

www.maritimepress.de | office@maritimepress.de

Bei diesem Titel handelt es sich um den Nachdruck eines historischen, lange vergriffenen Buches. Da elektronische Druckvorlagen für diese Titel nicht existieren, musste auf alte Vorlagen zurückgegriffen werden. Hieraus zwangsläufig resultierende Qualitätsverluste bitten wir zu entschuldigen.

## MARINE DIESEL ENGINE

MODELS: 4D242; 4D254; 6D363; 6D363TC; 6D380

# OPERATORS MANUAL AND PARTS IDENTIFICATION

**Lehman Power Corporation**
226 West Park Place Newark, Delaware 19711
Telephone (302) 454 7300. Telex 6853185 Lehmn UW.

**Sabre Lehman Power Limited,** Ferndown Industrial Estate,
22 Cobham Road, Wimborne, Dorset BH21 7PW.
Telephone: 01202 893720   Telex: 417269
Fax: 01202 872793.

# HOW TO USE THIS MANUAL

This manual is divided into sections as follows:

SECTION 1 - Page Nos. 1/up - General data, specifications, installation, adjustments, maintenance, etc. See index below.

SECTION A - Page Nos. A1/up - Parts identification of Ford base engines. See index on page A-1.

SECTION B - Page Nos. B1/up - Parts identification of Lehman marinizing parts. See index page B-1.

In order to provide a simple method of identification, all models included herein have been assigned a "code" letter as follows:

| ENGINE CODE | CU/IN | No. CYLS. | YEARS | IDENTIFICATION |
|---|---|---|---|---|
| E | 242 | 4 | 2/65 - 11/69 | With cylinder liners |
| F | 363 | 6 | 2/65 - 11/69 | With cylinder liners |
| G | 254 | 4 | 12/69 - up | Less cylinder liners |
| H | 380 | 6 | 12/69 - up | Less cylinder liners |
| I | 363 | 6 | 7/68 - up | Turbocharged |

## INSTRUCTIONS FOR ORDERING PARTS

Parts listed herein may be ordered through any Lehman Distributor, any Ford Industrial Engine Distributor or directly from the Lehman Power Corporation. Prices will be quoted upon request. In order to prevent errors, please order any required material by exact part number and name of part. Be sure to include engine model, serial number and year of manufacture, if known (see page 7). All orders must be accompanied by a deposit of one-third cost of material unless prior credit has been approved.

## INDEX - SECTION 1

| | |
|---|---|
| Air bleeding the fuel system | page 17 |
| Before operation | 14 |
| Bleeding the fuel system | 17 |
| Break-In | 14 |
| Controls | 14 |
| Cooling system | 19-21 |
| Dimensions, engine | 8 |
| Draining engine | 20-29 |
| Electrics | 22 |
| Fault-finding guide | 13-14 |
| Filters, fuel | 26 |
| Filters, air | 28 |
| Fuel system | 15-17 |
| Identification of models | 7 |
| Idling adjustment | 28 |
| Injectors (removal of) | 28 |
| Lift pump | 28 |
| Lubrication system | 23 |
| Maintenance | 26 |
| Minor repairs | 27 |
| Nameplate data | 7 |
| Oil recommendations | 23 |
| Power charts | 10-12 |
| Running -in | 14 |
| Specifications | 9 |
| Starting, stopping engine | 14 |
| Tachometer take-off | 23 |
| Timing the injection pump | 18 |
| Torque charts | 10-12 |
| Transmission | 25 |
| Trouble-shooting chart | 13-14 |
| Valve adjustments | 27 |
| Vee belt | 28 |
| Warranty | 4-6 |
| Water heater connection | 30 |
| Winterizing | 29 |
| Wiring diagram | 22 |

Copyright 1978 - LEHMAN POWER CORP., Linden, N.J.

Dear Engine Owner:

Welcome to the growing family of Lehman Power Marine diesel engine users. You'll be happy to know that you have chosen an engine which is heartily endorsed by leading boat builders for its quality, performance, fuel economy and long life. Your engine is simple but highly efficient. Its power, stamina and fuel economy will amaze you — especially if you've previously operated gasoline power.

To obtain the best performance and the longest life from any machine, it must be serviced properly and regularly. Filters should be changed, coolant checked, oil changed at specified times, etc. Follow the suggested schedule shown herein — it will add to your boating safety, economy and enjoyment.

Perhaps the most important single recommendation I can make to the new engine owner is "do not tinker"! If the unit is running well — leave it alone! Adjustments and repairs should be performed only by a competent diesel mechanic who has the proper knowledge and tools. Many times we are requested to assist an owner who has attempted his own repairs. Unless you know what you're doing, please "hands off"!

Lehman has a world-wide Service Network of Distributors and Dealers. Get to know your local one through the Lehman Start Up Program and they will be on hand to help you, should you need it.

Finally, always insist on genuine Lehman Parts. There are many examples of good boating days ruined by the use of spurious engine and cooling circuit parts. Always specify Lehman parts. If you have difficulty in obtaining them, please contact Lehman.

With proper care your Lehman Power engine will provide many hours of carefree boating. Thanks for the confidence you have shown in our Company by selecting our equipment. You will not be disappointed.

# 'Here's how to operate me...'

## ENGINE WARRANTY (LIMITED)

*Dear Engine Owner:*

The Lehman Power Corporation is fully aware of the problems which are sometimes encountered in obtaining service for marine powering equipment. We offer the following in an endeavor to provide an understanding of and solve such problems in the quickest and most efficient manner.

It should be recognized that servicing a marine engine cannot be compared to repairs to an automobile engine. In many cases the boat cannot be moved to a repair facility such as towing a car to a garage; breakdowns may occur in remote waters far from competent mechanics and spare parts; the yard or marina at which a disabled boat is berthed may not have qualified mechanics and, of course, marine facilities are far fewer in number than auto repair garages. Facilities and mechanics to service marine engines are usually limited to the immediate area in which boats are moored. The reasonable boat owner cannot expect the same service which may be available to him in case of an emergency auto repair. An impatient boatman may well become frustrated if he attempts to compare available service facilities between the marine and auto industries.

Your Lehman *Econ-O-Power* engine is built using a Ford engine as the "base" unit. Lehman manufactures and provides the "conversion" equipment .... those parts which are needed to adapt the Ford engine to marine use. In many instances, Lehman provides these parts to "engine converters" who assemble them to Ford engines purchased locally. Sometimes Lehman provides only a portion of the complete conversion with the converter supplying the balance of required parts. Lehman may also provide the completed engine which is fitted with the *Econ-O-Power* conversion equipment at the Lehman factory.

But, your base engine is warranted by Ford Motor Company regardless of where or who converted it .... if the conversion is an approved type such as Lehman equipment. Lehman warrants the parts manufactured and supplied by them. Claims for service or parts under warranty should be directed to either your nearest Ford distributor or to the Lehman Power Corporation (or Lehman distributor) depending upon the nature of the complaint. The two applicable warranties and extent of coverage follows.

Be assured we will work with you to the fullest extent in order to service your requirements.

*Lehman Power Corporation*

# FORD MOTOR WARRANTY (LIMITED)

This warranty covers the base engine as provided by Ford - cylinder assembly from rocker arm cover to engine base and from flywheel to front water pump. Starting motor and complete fuel system (including fuel transfer pump, injectors, injection pump, fuel filter, etc.) are included.

Warranty claims should be directed to your nearest Ford Industrial Products Distributor. There are many such distributors throughout the U.S. (Any Ford dealer will advise your nearest contact) and these companies often have dealers in areas which they cannot efficiently service themselves. If in doubt regarding any warranty problem, or if complete satisfaction is not obtained, contact Lehman Power Corporation
The following excerpts are from the standard Ford warranty as applies to marine power applications. But, please note that this summary is not complete and, of course, is subject to change:

"Ford Motor Company warrants that each part of such engine will be free under normal use and service from defects in material and workmanship for a period of one year from the date of delivery to the original retail purchaser. In the event that new Ford base engine assemblies are used in marine power commercial or work boat applications, each part of such engine will be free under normal use and service from defects in material and workmanship for a period of six months from the date of delivery to the original retail purchaser. Ford's obligation is limited to free replacement of, including related labor (other than labor required to remove, replace or gain access to the engine) at a Ford approved location or credit for such parts as shall be returned to Ford with transportation prepaid and as shall be acknowledged by Ford to be defective.

This warranty shall not apply to any Ford engine 1) if it has been subject to misapplication, abuse, misuse, negligence or accident, or 2) if parts not made or supplied by Ford have been used in connection with it if, in the sole judgement of Ford, such use affects its performance, stability, or reliability 3) if it has been altered or repaired outside of a Ford location in a manner which, in the sole judgement of Ford affects its performance, stability or reliability, or 4) if it shows evidence of participation in racing or other competitive activities."

A warranty registration form is provided with your engine. Before placing engine in service, complete all questions and forward all copies, excepting the one marked "owner" to:

    Ford Motor Company - Engine & Foundry Division
    Industrial Engine & Turbine Operations
    P.O. Box 1796    Village Plaza
    Dearborn, Michigan    48121

The "Owner" copy should be kept by the engine owner in case it should be required for reference or proof of registration.

## LEHMAN DIESEL ENGINE WARRANTY (LIMITED)

Complete diesel engines provided by Lehman Power Corporation are fully checked and tested prior to shipment. An occasional defect will become apparent only after the equipment has been placed in service and, in such cases, defective parts will be replaced under the terms of our standard warranty as follows:

"The manufacturer warrants each new assembly or component part manufactured by him to be free from defects in material and workmanship when used by the original purchaser under normal conditions for the purpose and service for which intended.

Under this warranty, such material claimed defective may be returned to the factory not longer than one (1) year after date of purchase. Upon inspection by the manufacturer and verification by him of defects claimed, the manufacturer will at his option repair or replace such material at no charge.

Diesel engines provided by Lehman include a Lehman warranty card which must be completed and mailed prior to or at time of initial engine "start-up" in order to initiate warranty. No claims will be honored unless such registration has been filed.

The manufacturer will not be responsible for time spent, work performed or materials furnished by others without his written authorization."

It is recognized that, in practice, it is often impractical to remove some vital part from the engine and await its delivery to our factory, repair and return to service. Therefor, if a defective part becomes apparent, the user may notify us and a replacement will be forwarded at once. Such replacement part must be paid for at time of delivery. If the part claimed defective is returned to the Lehman Power Corporation within thirty (30) days of receipt of replacement and if defect is confirmed, customer will be issued credit on the purchased part. If found not defective, part will be returned to customer and no credit issued.

A defective Lehman part is our responsibility and we realize that labor charges will be incurred in making required replacement. Lehman will absorb such costs, within the limits shown below, on defective parts removed from engines which have been assembled, tested and provided complete from the Lehman factory for marine installation. Please note that these charges will not be reimbursed on those installations where basic engines or transmissions are provided by others. It is only through assembly and testing and final inspection of the complete engine "package" within our plant that hidden defects may become apparent.

When applicable under above conditions, allowable labor time will be as follows: (Time shown is for re-removal of defective part, replacement and paint, if required.)

| | |
|---|---|
| Alternator assembly | one half hour |
| Engine mount (and align engine) | one hour |
| Oil cooler (engine or transmission) | one hour |
| Heat exchanger | one hour |
| Exhaust manifold (4 cyl. model) | two and one quarter hours |
| Exhaust manifold (6 cyl. models) | two and one half hours |
| Transmission | three hours |
| Expansion tank | one half hour |

All warranty claims must be accompanied by engine serial number, name of boat manufacturer with model and serial numbers, name and address of owner, date engine placed in service and full history of defect.

### EXCLUSIONS

This warranty shall not apply to:
- a) Failure resulting from improper installation of engine.
- b) Failure resulting from lack of proper maintenance.
- c) Engines used for racing or operated in excess of rated speed.
- d) Cost of removal or reinstallation in a boat.
- e) Engines which may have been operated with improper or contaminated fuel or lubricants.
- f) Engines which are installed in such manner that servicing or parts replacement cannot be normally accomplished.
- g) Any engine which has been altered or adjusted so as to impair its original characteristics.

## MODEL IDENTIFICATION & SERIAL NUMBERS

The model and serial number of your engine is easily located by reference to the following drawing. It will be noted that an identification plate with detailed information is affixed to the flywheel housing (starting May, 1972) at approximately the 2 o'clock position. Serial number is also stamped on a "pad" located at front, right side of engine block (behind water hose). The cubic inch displacement of engine is stamped on similar pad at rear of block, right side.

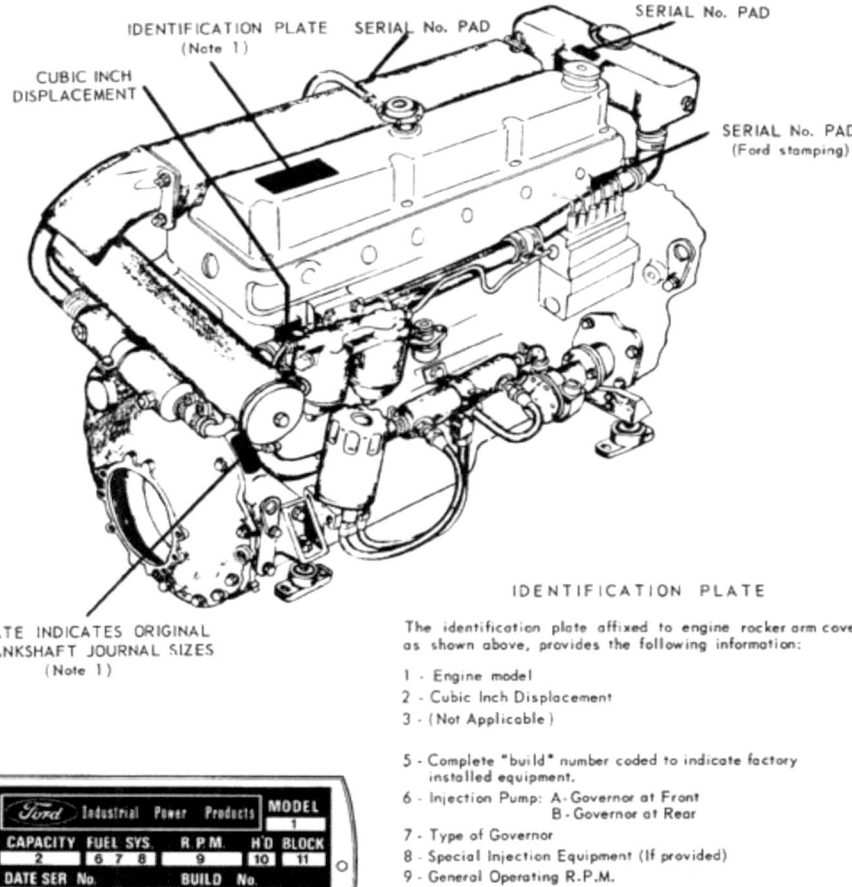

### IDENTIFICATION PLATE

The identification plate affixed to engine rocker arm cover as shown above, provides the following information:

1 - Engine model
2 - Cubic Inch Displacement
3 - (Not Applicable)

5 - Complete "build" number coded to indicate factory installed equipment.
6 - Injection Pump: A - Governor at Front
    B - Governor at Rear
7 - Type of Governor
8 - Special Injection Equipment (If provided)
9 - General Operating R.P.M.
10 - Cylinder Head Type
11 - Engine Block Type
12 - Special Equipment (If provided)

Note 1: Prior to mid-1977, identification plate was located on flywheel housing.

## INSTALLATION DIMENSIONS

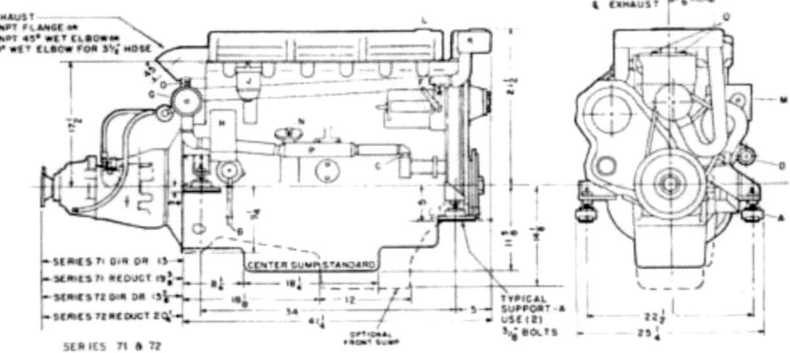

6 CYLINDER MODELS

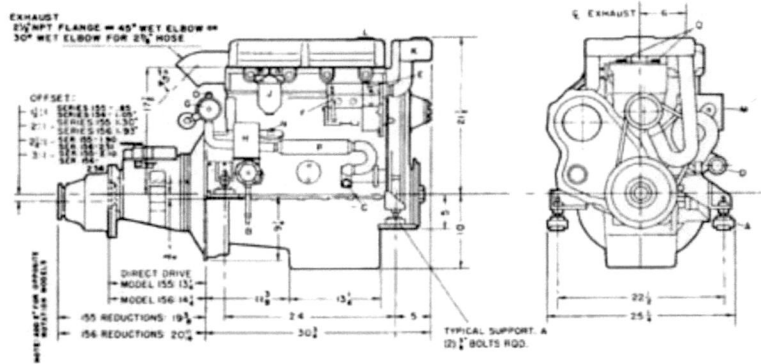

4 CYLINDER MODELS

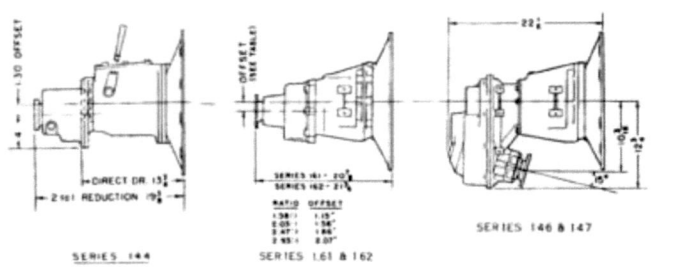

TRANSMISSIONS

A - Typical Support (4)
B - Fuel Inlet 5/16" tube
C - Raw Water In - 3/4" npt
D - Starter Solenoid
E - Engine stop control
F - Throttle control
G - Heat Exchanger clean-out
H - Oil Filter
J - Fuel Filter
K - Fresh Water Tank
L - Oil Fill Cap
M - Air Filter
N - Tach. Adaptor, 2:1, CCW
O - Zinc Pencil
P - Lube Oil Cooler
Q - Temp. gage connection

Key to above drawings

## SPECIFICATIONS

| | G - 254 cu/in. 4 Cyl. | H - 380 cu/in. 6 Cyl. | I - 363 6 Cyl. Turbo. |
|---|---|---|---|
| TYPE | \.\.\.\.\.\.\. 4 CYCLE, OVERHEAD VALVE, DIRECT INJECTION \.\.\.\.\.\.\. | | |
| MODEL (INDUSTRIAL) | 2712-E | 2715-E | 2704-ET |
| MODEL (LEHMAN) | 4D254 | 6D380 | 6D363T |
| BORE x STROKE | 4.22 × 4.52" | 4.22 × 4.52" | 4.125 × 4.52" |
| CAPACITY | 254 cu/in. (4150 cc) | 380 cu/in. (6220 cc) | 363 cu/in. (5950 cc) |
| B.H.P. (B.S. Overload) | 80 at 2500 rpm | 120 at 2500 rpm | 150 at 2400 rpm |
| (Cont. B Din. 6270) | 74.2 at 2500 rpm | 114.5 at 2500 rpm | 136.5 at 2400 rpm |
| TORQUE (B.S. Overload) | 186 ft/lbs at 1600 rpm | 280 ft/lbs at 1600 rpm | 348 ft/lbs at 1800 rpm |
| (B.S. Rating) | 168 ft/lbs at 1600 rpm | 252 ft/lbs at 1600 rpm | 317 ft/lbs at 1800 rpm |
| COMPRESSION RATIO | 16 to 1 | 16 to 1 | 15.7 to 1 |
| COMPRESSION PRESSURE | \.\.\.\.\.\.\. 360 lbs. per sq. in. at 215 rpm \.\.\.\.\.\.\. | | |
| FIRING ORDER | 1-2-4-3 | 1-5-3-6-2-4 | 1-5-3-6-2-4 |
| CRANKSHAFT ROTATION | \.\.\.\.\.\.\. C.C.W. facing flywheel \.\.\.\.\.\.\. | | |
| MAX. INSTALLATION ANGLE | *15° | *15° | 15° |
| GOVERNED SPEED (Max) NO LOAD | 2650 rpm | 2650 rpm | 2500 rpm |
| UNDER LOAD | 2500 rpm | 2500 rpm | 2400 rpm |
| IDLING SPEED | \.\.\.\.\.\.\. 600 - 700 rpm \.\.\.\.\.\.\. | | |
| EXHAUST SIZE | 2 1/2" NPT | 3" NPT | 4" I.D. Hose |
| EXHAUST BACK PRESSURE (Max) | \.\.\.\.\.\.\. 1½ lb/sq.in.(3.0" Mercury) \.\.\.\.\.\.\. | | .491 lb/sq.in.(1.0" Hg) |
| COLD START | Excess fuel device | Excess fuel device | Glow plug |
| FUEL | No. 2 Diesel | No. 2 Diesel | No. 2 Diesel |
| VALVES | \.\.\.\.\.\.\. Free turn type \.\.\.\.\.\.\. | | |
| VALVE CLEARANCE (hot) | Int. .015"; Exh. .012" | Int. .015"; Exh. .012" | Int. .018"; Exh. .018" |
| PISTONS | \.\.\.\.\.\.\. Aluminum alloy, tin plated \.\.\.\.\.\.\. | | |
| COMBUSTION CHAMBER | \.\.\.\.\.\.\. Machined in piston crown \.\.\.\.\.\.\. | | |
| PISTON RINGS | \.\.\.\.\.\.\. 3 Compression; 1 Oil control \.\.\.\.\.\.\. | | |
| CAMSHAFT | \.\.\.\.\.\.\. Cast iron alloy; Gear driven \.\.\.\.\.\.\. | | |
| CRANKSHAFT | \.\.\.\.\.\.\. Steel forging \.\.\.\.\.\.\. | | |
| MAIN BEARINGS | 5 | 7 | 7 |
| LUBE SYSTEM: | | | |
| OIL CAPACITY (level, w/filter) | 8 qts. | 12 qts. | 12 qts. |
| NORMAL OIL PRESSURE | \.\.\.\.\.\.\. 30 lbs/sq. in. at 1600 rpm; 35 lbs/sq. in. at 2000 rpm \.\.\.\.\.\.\. | | |
| OIL TEMPERATURE (range) | \.\.\.\.\.\.\. 165 - 220° \.\.\.\.\.\.\. | | |
| LUBRICANT | | | |
| Above 90°f | | | |
| 20 to 90°f | See pages 23 - 24 | | |
| Below 30°f | | | |
| OIL FILTER | \.\.\.\.\.\.\. Full flow, disposable, "spin-on" type \.\.\.\.\.\.\. | | Cannister type |
| OIL COOLER | \.\.\.\.\.\.\. Shell and tube type heat exchanger \.\.\.\.\.\.\. | | |
| FUEL INJECTION PUMP | \.\.\.\.\.\.\. Simms, multi-element \.\.\.\.\.\.\. | | |
| GOVERNOR | Mechanical | Mechanical | Mechanical |
| TIMING | 20° BTDC No.1 piston | 20° BTDC No.1 piston | 23° BTDC No.1 piston |
| LUBRICANT | \.\.\.\.\.\.\. Same as engine sump \.\.\.\.\.\.\. | | |
| OIL CAPACITY | .75 pints | .90 pints | .90 pints |
| INJECTORS | \.\.\.\.\.\.\. 4 hole type \.\.\.\.\.\.\. | | |
| OPENING PRESSURE | 182.5 to 187.5 Atmos. | 182.5 to 187.5 Atmos. | 203 to 209 Atmos. |
| FUEL LIFT PUMP | \.\.\.\.\.\.\. Diaphragm with hand priming lever \.\.\.\.\.\.\. | | |
| COOLING SYSTEM | \.\.\.\.\.\.\. Pressurized, series type \.\.\.\.\.\.\. | | |
| CAPACITY, WATER | 15 quarts | 20 quarts | 20 quarts |
| OPERATING TEMP. | \.\.\.\.\.\.\. 175 - 190°f. (79 - 88°c) \.\.\.\.\.\.\. | | |
| OPTIMUM TEMP. | \.\.\.\.\.\.\. 195°f. (90°c) \.\.\.\.\.\.\. | | |
| CIRCULATION | \.\.\.\.\.\.\. 35.3 GPM at 2400 engine rpm \.\.\.\.\.\.\. | | |
| ELECTRICAL SYSTEM | \.\.\.\.\.\.\. 12 volt; negative ground \.\.\.\.\.\.\. | | |
| ALTERNATOR | \.\.\.\.\.\.\. 55 Amps. with integral voltage regulator \.\.\.\.\.\.\. | | |
| SUGGESTED BATTERY | \.\.\.\.\.\.\. 140 amp./hr. minimum \.\.\.\.\.\.\. | | |
| STARTING MOTOR | \.\.\.\.\.\.\. 2 stage, pre-engage type \.\.\.\.\.\.\. | | |
| VOLTS | 12 | 12 | 12 |
| LOCK TORQUE | \.\.\.\.\.\.\. 37.5 ft/lbs., 1070 amp. draw \.\.\.\.\.\.\. | | |
| RUNNING TORQUE | \.\.\.\.\.\.\. 18.6 at 1000 rpm; 650 amp. draw \.\.\.\.\.\.\. | | |
| HEAT EXCHANGER | \.\.\.\.\.\.\. Shell and tube type, 2 pass \.\.\.\.\.\.\. | | |
| RAW WATER PUMP | \.\.\.\.\.\.\. Bronze, single impeller type, gear driven \.\.\.\.\.\.\. | | |
| MANIFOLD, EXHAUST | \.\.\.\.\.\.\. Gray iron, fresh water cooled \.\.\.\.\.\.\. | | |
| MANIFOLD, INTAKE | Integral with exhaust | Integral with exhaust | Separate |
| AIR FILTER ELEMENT | \.\.\.\.\.\.\. Polyurethane, 40 pore, replaceable \.\.\.\.\.\.\. | | Wire Mesh |
| ENGINE MOUNTINGS | \.\.\.\.\.\.\. Rubber compound, adjustable \.\.\.\.\.\.\. | | |
| FUEL LINE | \.\.\.\.\.\.\. 3/8" Recommended. Reduce to 5/16" at engine \.\.\.\.\.\.\. | | |
| TACHOMETER ADAPTOR | \.\.\.\.\.\.\. Turns C.C.W. at 1/2 engine speed. Adapts to 7/8" - 18 ferrule \.\.\.\.\.\.\. | | |
| FAN BELT TENSION | \.\.\.\.\.\.\. 1/2" free movement \.\.\.\.\.\.\. | | |
| WEIGHTS: | | | |
| ENGINE (Less transmission) | 874 lbs. | 1092 lbs. | 1120 lbs. |
| BLOCK ONLY | 230 lbs. | 340 lbs. | 360 lbs. |
| HEAD with VALVES | 82 lbs. | 120 lbs. | 120 lbs. |
| FLYWHEEL | 87 lbs. | 87 lbs. | 87 lbs. |

* 15° with standard sump. 18° with front well type sump.

# 4 CYLINDER, 254 Cu./In., LEHMAN MODEL 4D254

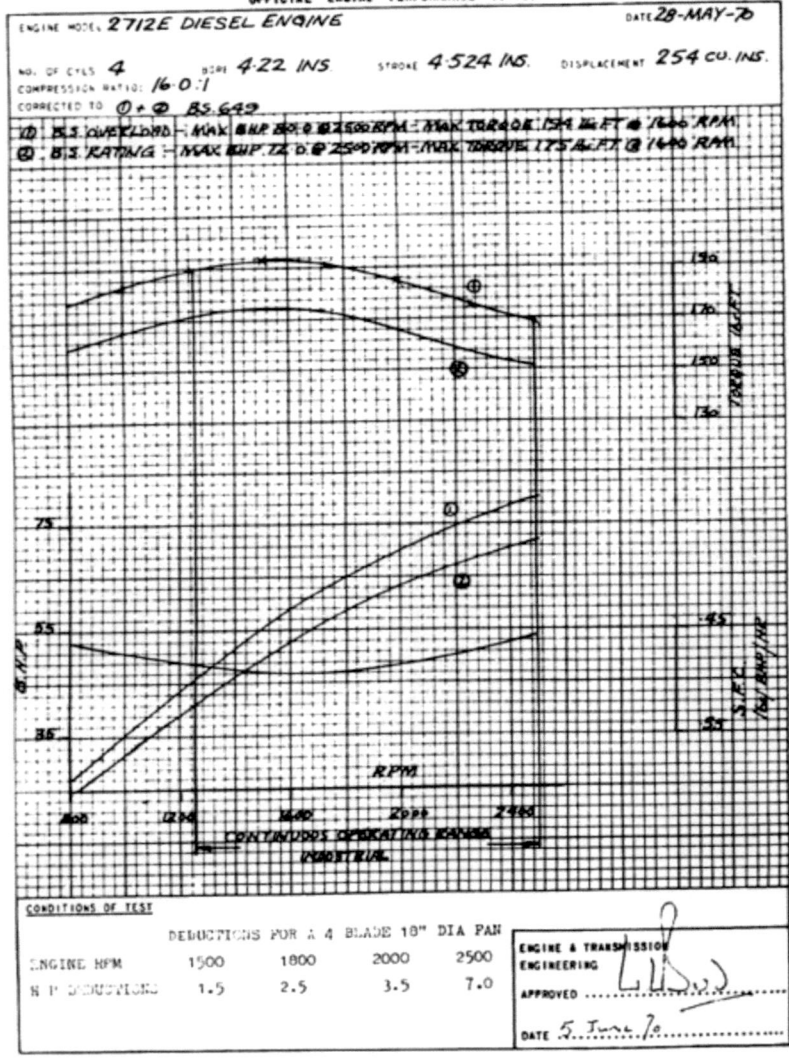

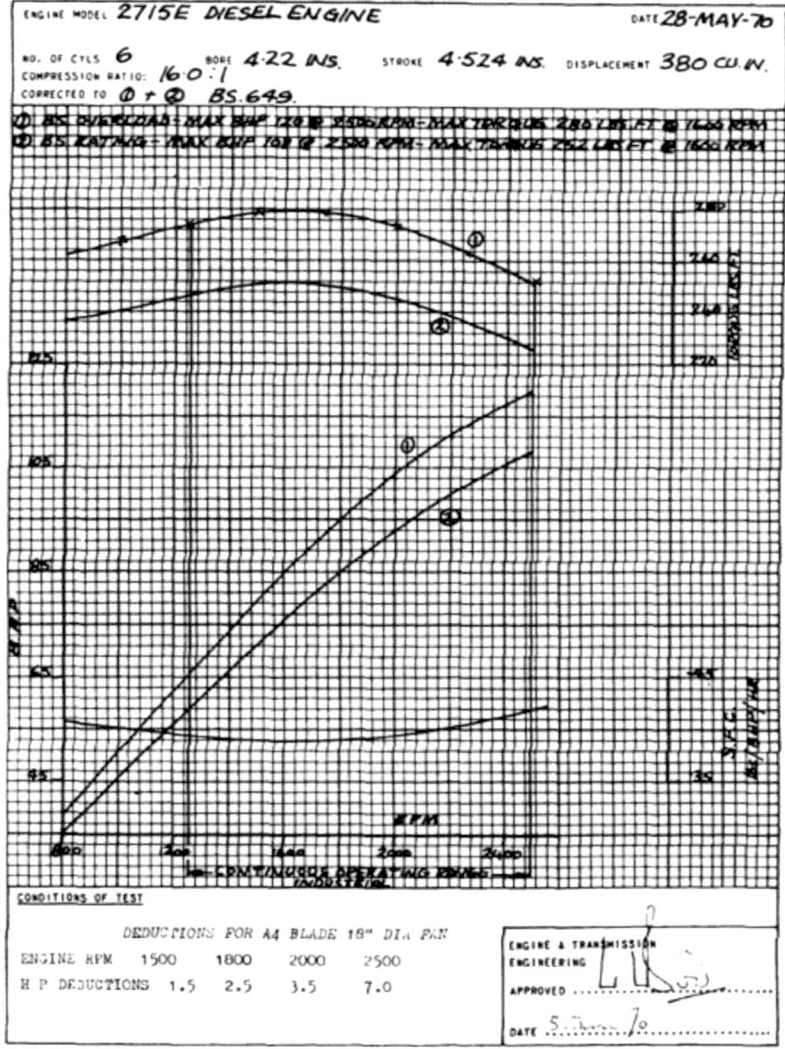

# 6 CYLINDER, 363 Cu./In. TURBOCHARGED - LEHMAN MODEL 6D363TC

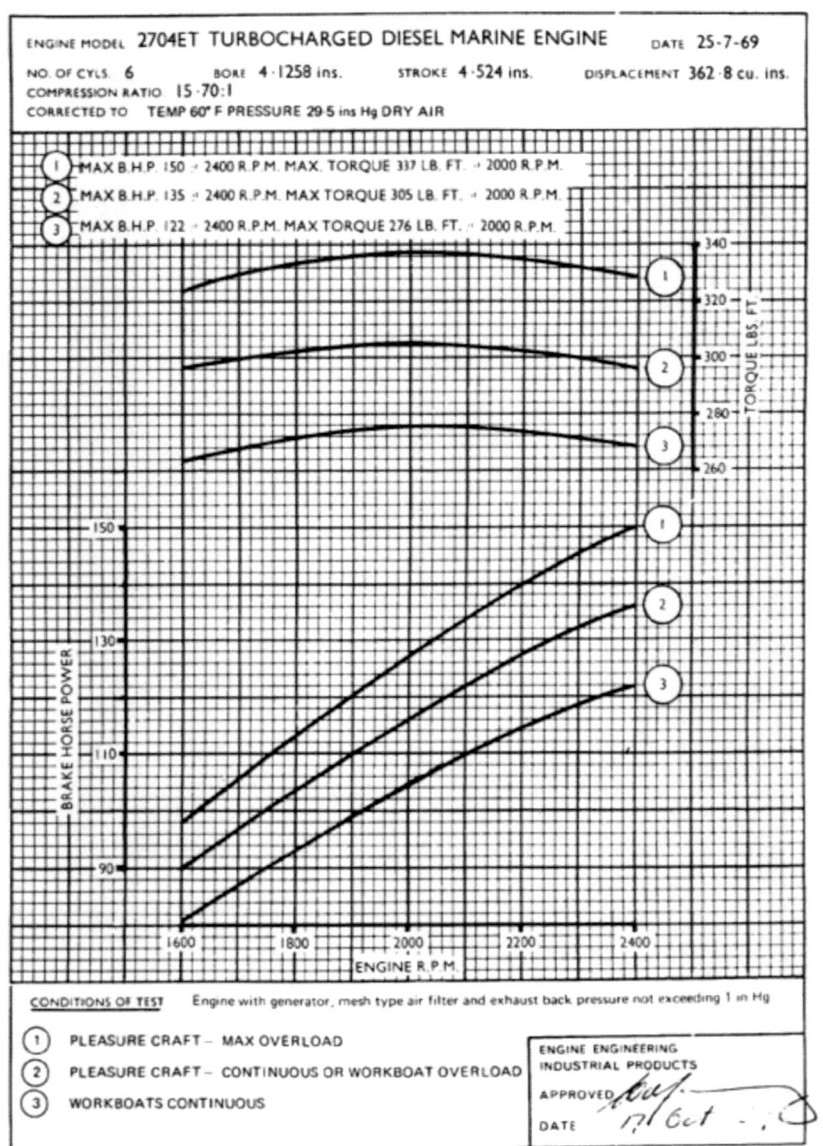

## LEHMAN DIESEL OWNERS' FAULT-FINDING GUIDE

\* Particular attention should be directed to the most common trouble-spots marked by asterik -

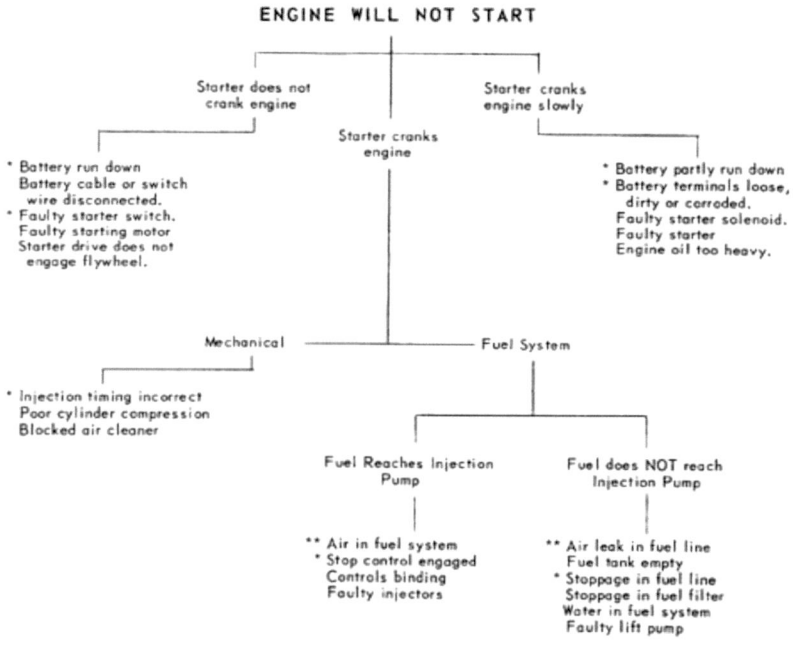

### ENGINE STARTS

**ENGINE RUNS INTERMITTENTLY**

   Idle adjustment too low
\* Air - Leaking fuel system
   Fuel (lift) pump diaphragm worn
   Fuel tank near empty
   Fuel filter(s) clogged

**ROUGH IDLING**

\* Air in fuel system
\* Idle adjustment set too low
\* Idle damper screw requires adjustment
   Dirty or faulty injectors
   Injector pipes loose, cracked or broken
   Incorrect injection timing

**ENGINE NOT DELIVERING FULL POWER**

\*\* Air in fuel system
   Engine overheated
   Injection timing incorrect
   Incorrect valve clearances
   Dirty air cleaner(s)
   Stop control partly engaged

**ENGINE KNOCKS**

\* Air in fuel system
   Oil level (pressure) low
   Incorrect grade fuel oil
   Water - Leaking cylinder head gasket
   Incorrect injection timing
   Faulty injector
   Sticking valve or rocker arm

Continued on following page . . . .

## FAULT-FINDING GUIDE (Continued)

### ENGINE OVERHEATS

* Insufficient water supply
  Fresh water not circulating
  a) Loose or broken vee belt
  b) Hoses clogged or collapsing
     while running at high speed.
  c) Faulty thermostat
* d) Air trapped in water system.
* e) Clogged heat exchanger
  f) Clogged bleed hole in thermostat
  Sea water flow insufficient
* a) Clogged sea water strainer
  b) Water intake scoop damaged or lost
  c) Sea cock closed
  d) Water pump impeller damaged
* e) Heat exchanger or oil coolers clogged.
  Low crankcase oil level
  Incorrect injection timing

### ENGINE EXHAUST SMOKES

Fuel, poor grade (black smoke)
Crankcase overfilled (blue smoke)
Cold engine temperature (white or lite blue)
* Propeller too large (black smoke)
  Max. speed stop screw set too high
  for load (black smoke)
  Propeller too small (white smoke)
  Excess fuel button stuck
  Incorrect injection timing

### ENGINE MISFIRES

* Injector pipe loose, broken or cranked
  Injectors dirty
* Air leaking in fuel system
  Sticking valve or rocker arm

## BEFORE OPERATION

Before operating a new engine it should be thoroughly inspected for damage likely to affect its subsequent operation or that may have resulted from shipment or installation in the boat. Controls should be inspected to assure best perform properly and, of course, the operator should be familiar with all controls, instruments and proper engine operation.

The engine should not be started until the operator has read this manual thoroughly and familiarized himself with manner of checking oil level in engine sump, coolant level, oil in injection pump sump, oil in transmission, bleeding of air from fuel system, etc. The chapters on "maintenance" and "running in" should be particularly noted.

Assuming that all engine checks have been performed you are ready to start your engine.

**IMPORTANT**
Before starting turbo engine, refer to "Lubrication" section for information regarding priming with oil.

## RUNNING IN

DO NOT OPERATE YOUR NEW ENGINE AT HIGH SPEEDS IMMEDIATELY' FOR EXCESSIVE WEAR OR DAMAGE MAY RESULT.

Long and dependable service may be expected if proper care is taken during the "break-in" period. The following speed limitations are recommended:

| RUNNING TIME | RPM |
|---|---|
| 30 Minutes | Idle (no load) |
| 30 Minutes | 800 |
| 1 Hour | 1000 |
| 1 Hour | 1200 |
| 2 Hours | 1400 |
| 4 Hours | 1500 |

Total run-in period — 9 hours
After the first 15 hours, complete the maintenance instructions as shown elsewhere in this manual.

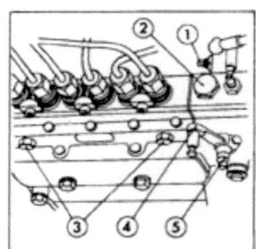

FIG. 2
INJECTION PUMP
1 - Idling speed adj. screw
2 - Oil fill plug
3 - Air bleed screws
4 - Stop control lever
5 - Excess fuel (cold weather start) button.

## CONTROLS, STARTING & STOPPING ENGINE

No amount of engineering ingenuity or care in manufacture can substitute for the need of knowledge on the operation and avoidance of mis-use by the operator. It is important to be familiar with all controls so as to know how to properly operate your engine.

Refer to Fig. 2. To stop engine, the stop lever should be moved as far as it will travel towards the front of engine and held until engine is fully stopped. This lever cuts off the supply of fuel to the injection pump. (NOTE: Before shutting down engine it should always be allowed to idle for about two minutes, particularly after extended periods of cruising.)

Engine speed control is the longer lever at side of injection pump (Fig. 3). Moving toward front of engine increases engine speed.

The excess fuel device permits additional fuel to be supplied by the injection pump when starting engine in cold climates. It is situated in front of pump at base of engine stop lever. To operate, move throttle control lever to maximum engine speed position, push the excess fuel button inwards, then return throttle to about mid-point position. The button will spring out automatically when engine starts. Do not attempt to wedge the button in as this will reduce engine power.

FIG. 3
INJECTION PUMP DETAIL
1 - Throttle control lever (at maximum speed position.)
2 - Excess fuel (cold weather start) button.

To start engine when cold — make certain that transmission is in neutral position and that all boat accessory equipment (bilge pump, extra alternator or generator, hydraulic pump, winch, etc.) is disengaged. Check that engine stop lever is fully towards rear (flywheel end) of engine. Set throttle lever to ¼ open position. (In extreme cold weather, engage the excess fuel device as described above.) Press starting button to operate starter. As soon as engine starts, release starting button and reduce speed control lever to warm-up (idling) speed of 700-800 RPM. If engine fails to start within 5 seconds, release starting button. Try again after allowing sufficient time for all moving parts to stop.

Once engine has started, it should be allowed to reach 170°F before full load is applied.

To restart engine when warm, use same procedure as above except set speed control lever to approximately mid-point of its travel.

## FUEL SYSTEM

Caution: Your injection pump is a very accurately machined piece of equipment and requires careful handling and adjustment. No repairs other than shown herein should be entrusted to other than a diesel repair facility having the required tools, knowledge and test calibration equipment.

Caution: Never bend the injector pipes (which connect injection pump to injectors) as this may unbalance the volume of fuel delivered to each cylinder.

Caution: Do not use a galvanized fuel tank as the zinc coating reacts with the fuel oil and forms undesirable compounds which can foul the injection system.

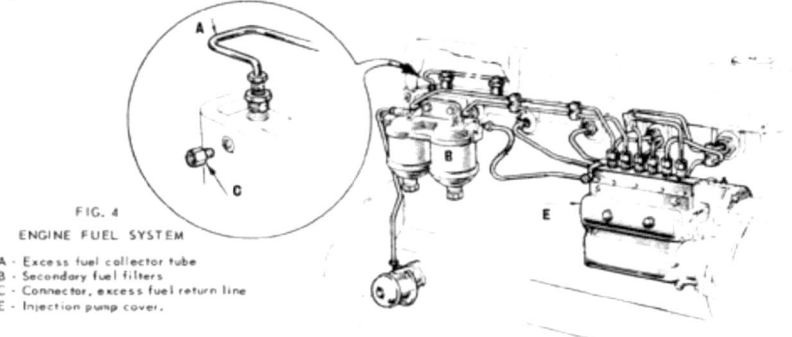

FIG. 4
ENGINE FUEL SYSTEM
A - Excess fuel collector tube
B - Secondary fuel filters
C - Connector, excess fuel return line
E - Injection pump cover.

## FUEL SYSTEM (Continued)

The fuel injection equipment is made to very accurate limits and therefore even the smallest particle of dirt entering the system will destroy its efficiency by causing blockage or scoring or premature wear on highly finished parts. A clean fuel system is absolutely essential. Insure scrupulous cleanliness when handling fuel or fuel system components. At all times make certain that water is not allowed to contaminate the fuel oil. Try to make a practice of refueling out of the rain. Use a fine gauze filter funnel and always wipe the fuel tank around the filler cap before and after filling and immediately replace the cap.

An efficient, large size primary fuel filter and water separator (colescer) is deemed a necessity in order to prevent foreign particles reaching the injection equipment on your engine.

Your engine is equipped with secondary fuel filters which filter out contaminates that may find their way through the primary filter. These filters (see fig. 4, 5 & 5-A) located towards rear of engine block, right side, have elements which should be replaced once each season or at least each 200 hours (whichever comes first) under normal conditions. (When replacing filters, use new gaskets or sealing rings to prevent air leaks.) Following filter replacement, bleed air from fuel system as later described under "bleeding the fuel system". Excess fuel delivered to the injectors by the injection pump is collected by a tube located under the rocker arm cover (see A, Fig. 4) and delivered to fitting C, Fig. 4 located at rear, right side of cylinder head. This fitting should be connected to top of fuel tank by ¼" (min.) tube or hose (C, Fig. 5) in order to return excess fuel to tank. Make sure to install a short section of flexible tubing in this line to prevent breakage due to engine vibration.

An overflow tube is provided on the sump of some injection pumps to prevent overfilling. Upon first filling or when replenishing oil, a can or other container may be used to catch the overflow oil until level in sump is balanced. If the injection pump does not have an overflow tube, it will have an oil level plug directly below the side cover E, Fig. 4. When adding oil, fill to level of this plug. An injection pump without overflow tube will have a vent containing a gauze filter which should be removed after each 200 hours of operation, washed in solvent such as kerosene, dipped in clean engine oil and replaced. In new installations, injection pump level should be watched carefully. A small amount of oil ejected from the overflow tube is no cause for concern, but indicates that sump may have been overfilled or oil is seeking a new level due to angle of installation. But should oil flow persist or if oil must be added between normal maintenance periods, such fact should be reported at once. Warranty does not cover injection pumps which have been operated without proper lubrication.

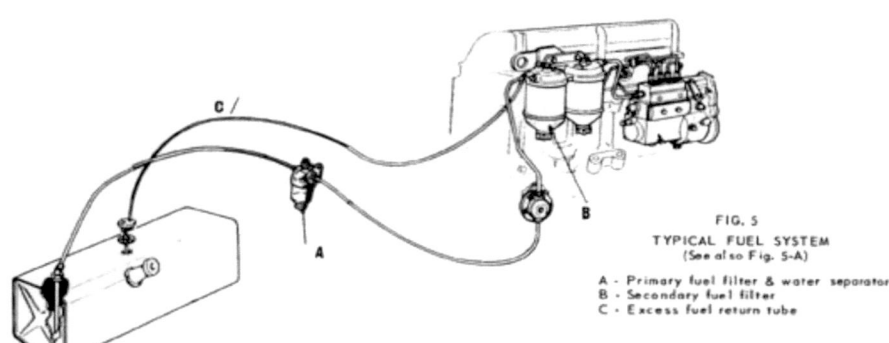

FIG. 5
TYPICAL FUEL SYSTEM
(See also Fig. 5-A)

A - Primary fuel filter & water separator
B - Secondary fuel filter
C - Excess fuel return tube

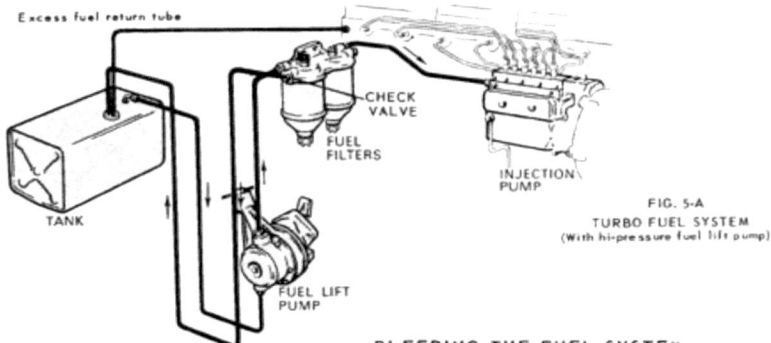

FIG. 5-A
TURBO FUEL SYSTEM
(With hi-pressure fuel lift pump)

## BLEEDING THE FUEL SYSTEM

Bleeding air from the fuel system may well be one of the important procedures to be learned by the operator. Air in the injection system may cause erratic engine performance, "missing" on one or more cylinders, reduced power, stop fuel from reaching engine and prevent or cause hard engine starting.

It must be remembered that the lift pump draws fuel from the tank, so any accumulation of air in the fuel system makes all connections, filters, etc. between fuel lift pump and tank suspect. In any new installation one must "bleed" the system of air for, obviously, air will be in the new fuel lines, filters, etc. If the fuel tank should run dry, bleeding will be needed when the boat is refueled. Bleeding will also be required after changing fuel filter elements. (Time and effort may be saved if filter is charged with fuel by removing the bleed plugs on top and slowly pouring fuel into the filter until it overflows.) Occasionally, after an extended run, an engine may slow down, or "miss", or lose RPM's or stop. Although there may be other causes, air in the fuel system should not be overlooked. Many times a tiny leak in a fuel line fitting may allow air to enter the system and accumulate until there is sufficient to cause the above mentioned symptoms.

Upon completing a new installation, best check against air leaks is to block the fuel tank vent and filler cap, disconnect fuel line at tank side of fuel lift pump and induct pressure (approximately 10 lbs. should suffice) into the fuel line. Make certain that fuel line to tank will maintain pressure and inspect all connections for possible leaks.

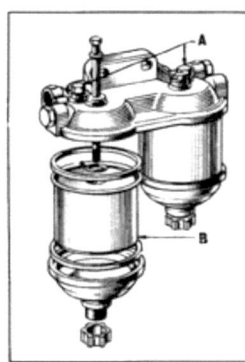

FIG. 6
FUEL FILTER (DUAL TYPE)
A - Bleed screws
B - Replaceable element

To bleed system, follow this procedure:

1. Ascertain that there is sufficient fuel in tank. (Note: Low fuel level may result in intake pipe being exposed due to "sloshing" of fuel, thus drawing air into system.

2. Make certain that fuel shut-off valve is turned on.

3. Loosen the bleed screw on the inlet side of the fuel filter (Fig. 6 & 7) about two or three turns.

4. Operate the priming lever at the side of the fuel lift pump (Fig. 8) until a flow of fuel, free of air, is expelled. Then close screw.

Caution: Do not use excess pressure in tightening bleed screws as the castings are soft and threads strip easily. A slight pressure with wrench will seal all plugs tightly.

Note: If the eccentric which operates the fuel lift pump is on maximum lift the pump priming lever will be inoperative. If this occurs, rotate the engine using starter until priming lever can be operated.

5. Loosen bleed screw on outlet side of filter and repeat operation 4.

6. Inspection of injection pump will reveal two additional bleed screws (Fig. 9). First loosen screw nearest to inlet line and repeat operation 4. The same procedure is then used on the last bleed screw.

Caution: Allow engine to operate for at least ten minutes before leaving dockside to ensure all air has been purged from system.

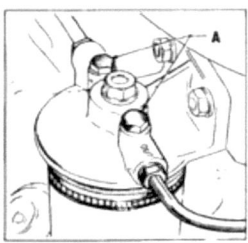

FIG. 7
FUEL FILTER (SINGLE TYPE)
A - Bleed screws

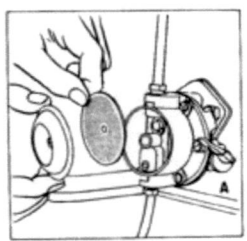

FIG. 8
FUEL LIFT PUMP
A - Priming lever

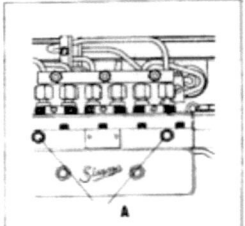

FIG. 9
INJECTION PUMP (TYPICAL)
A - Bleed screws

FIG. 10
INJECTION PUMP TIMING TOOL

## TIMING THE FUEL INJECTION PUMP

The injection pump delivers an accurately metered quantity of fuel to each cylinder to suit any engine speed and load condition. The pump is a very accurately machined piece of equipment and requires careful handling and maintenance. Repairs other than described in this manual should be entrusted only to a qualified diesel mechanic who is equipped with proper tools, gauges and test and setting equipment.

As indicated in the fault-finding chart, poor engine performance may sometimes be traced to incorrect injection timing. Following is the method to correctly set timing.

1. Position stop control lever to avoid starting engine.

2. Remove the inspection plug which is adjacent to the injection pump (Figure 10) and rotate engine crankshaft until the two semi-circular dimples which can be seen through the timing aperture are in line. (Note: Timing Tool No. C-9077 is available to insure positive location.)

3. It is now necessary to ascertain position of No. 1 piston. Two methods are possible . . . .

    a. Some models are equipped with a timing scale just forward of crankshaft pulley on port side (See Figure 11). Rotate engine crankshaft until timing mark (a saw cut or scratch mark) on periphery of pulley coincides with the desired mark on scale. See "Specifications".

    b. For engines not equipped with timing scale, it will be necessary to remove aperture cover on flywheel housing (in lower sector, starboard side) in order to check setting from markings on periphery of flywheel (See Figure 12). In marine use this may be difficult due to engine bed interference. A small mirror may be of assistance.

4. When crankshaft has been rotated to proper position, recheck the two "dimples" as per Paragraph 2. If not aligned, carefully loosen bolts holding injection pump to engine. Slotted holes in pump adaptor plate allows rotating pump to achieve proper alignment. Retighten bolts securely. (Note: If difficulty is experienced in rotating pump, disconnect injector pipes.)

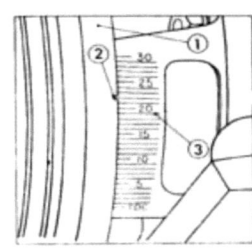

FIG. 11
ENGINE TIMING MARKS
1 - Crankshaft pulley
2 - Timing mark
3 - Timing scale

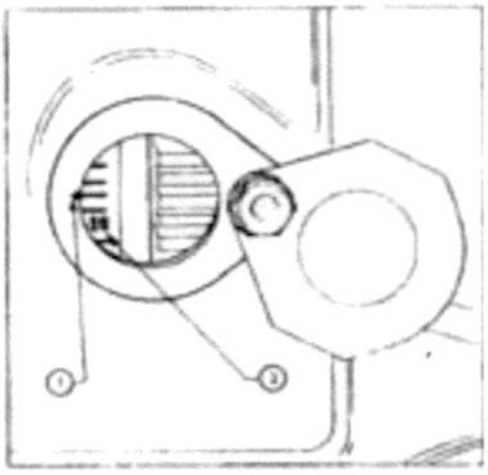

FIG. 12
TIMING MARKS (FLYWHEEL)
1 - Timing mark on engine flywheel housing.
2 - Timing scale on flywheel.

## COOLING SYSTEM

Your engine is cooled by the circulation of fresh water (contained in the system) through the water jackets surrounding the cylinders, cylinder head and exhaust manifold. The heated water flows by thermo-syphonic action, assisted by a pump at the front of cylinder block around the tubes of a "heat exchanger" located above the flywheel housing at rear of engine. Raw water from outside the boat flows through the heat exchanger tubes, and the heat from the fresh water is thus transferred to the raw water which is expelled overboard. Examination of Figures 13 and 14 will clarify the water systems. A thermostat located in front of cylinder head, below expansion tank, promotes rapid "warming up" and assists in maintaining constant engine temperature.

The fresh water system is filled through a cap atop the expansion tank at front of engine. Water level should be checked daily and maintained to within one-half inch below top of tank. The air bleed valve at top front end of exhaust manifold should be opened while filling fresh water system in order to allow trapped air to escape. When water appears, close valve tightly. DO NOT OPEN VALVE WHILE ENGINE IS RUNNING, as this will draw air into system, displacing water and causing overheating of engine.

> Most complaints of overheating are due to improper purging of air from the fresh water system. The following is correct method with engine not running:
>
> A. Open air bleed valve (on top front end of manifold) to allow air to escape.
> B. Remove filler cap from top of expansion tank.
> C. Slowly fill cooling system with water/anti-freeze mixture
> D. Continue filling cooling system until all air or bubbles cease to expel at air bleed valve, and solid stream of water appears.
> E. Close air bleed valve.
> F. Continue filling of cooling system until water level reaches top of expansion tank.
> G. Start engine and run approximately 900 RPM (in neutral) until thermostat opens. Turbulence in water will be noted through filler hole.
> H. Maintain water level to top of tank.
> I. Replace filler cap.
>
> DO NOT OPEN AIR BLEED VALVE WHILE ENGINE IS RUNNING, AS THIS WILL DRAW AIR INTO SYSTEM AND DISPLACE WATER AND CAUSE OVERHEATING.

The fresh water system is pressurized by the cap atop expansion tank. When proper pressure is reached, excess water is expelled through the overflow tube under tank. Extreme care should be taken in removing cap while engine is hot. While engine is hot, if there is liquid in tank, the system may be refilled with safety; if not, allow engine to cool before refilling. If an anti-freeze solution is not being used in freezing temperatures, it is essential that the water systems be drained while engine stands idle and refilled before engine is restarted. Check water supply daily. Maintain level to approximately one-half inch below top of tank.

To assist in corrosion control, a zinc pencil is installed in your heat exchanger at top, left side (6 cylinder models); bottom, left side in 4 cylinder models. This zinc pencil is sacrificial ... that is, the raw water will attack and "eat away" the zinc before attacking metal of the heat exchanger. It is suggested that the plug accommodating this pencil be removed each week while engine is in service in order to inspect zinc. Replace zinc element when required. Failure to install zincs when needed may cause serious damage to exchanger.

It will be noted that your heat exchanger has removable end caps to facilitate cleaning. Removing caps will allow access to end of the tube "bundle". To clean tubes use a 3/16" diameter wood dowel. Do not use a metal rod which may rupture the copper tubings.

FIG. 13 - FRESH WATER CIRCULATION SYSTEM

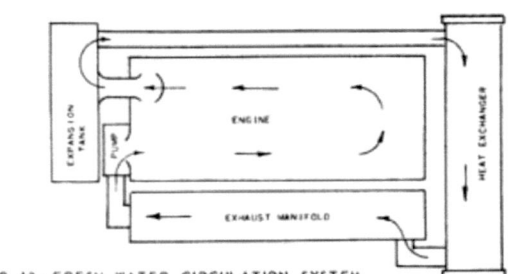

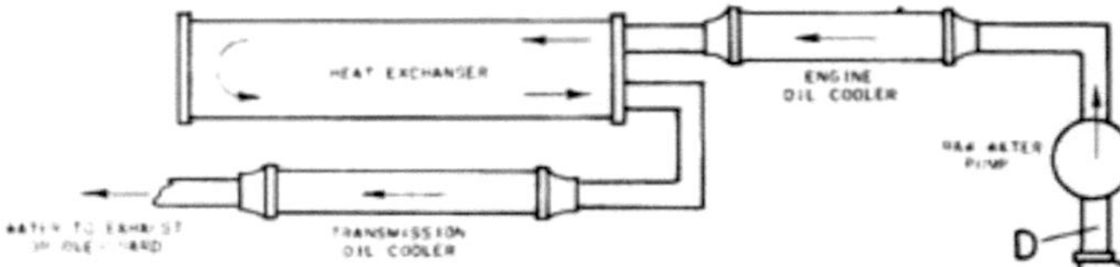

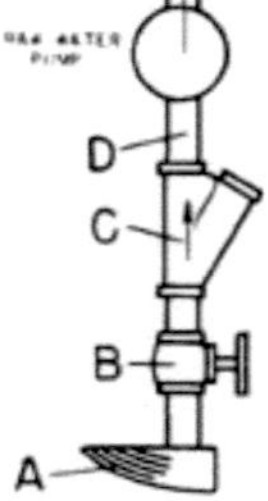

FIG. 14 - RAW WATER CIRCULATION SYSTEM

A - Intake scoop of standard marine design, minimum 1" NPT should be used for raw water inlet. Reduce to 3/4" NPT at pump. Recommended scoop has bars across opening to prevent entry of large pieces of foreign matter.

B - Sea-cock should be 1" NPT minimum size, "gate" type that opens fully to allow full, unrestricted flow of water.

C - The use of an efficient, full-flow raw water strainer is strongly recommended to prevent clogging of pump and exchangers by weeds, etc.

D - If hose is employed for intake, same should be reinforced type of extra heavy construction to prevent collapse under powerful suction of raw water pump.

In preparation for freezing weather, anti-freeze should be provided in the fresh water system of the engine. Due to the high temperatures at which these engines operate, high boiling point anti-freeze is demanded. Do not attempt to use alcohol or other non-permanent types, and do not use a "sealer" type which tends to build up a coating on exchanger elements, thus interfering with normal heat transfer. Consult the specification section of this manual to determine water capacity of your engine, and add sufficient anti-freeze to bring within limits of expected temperatures.

Inboard type heat exchangers must be drained of raw water when exposed to freezing temperatures. Raw water pump, water inlet piping and intake strainer should likewise be drained when subjected to extreme cold. Drains will be found at following locations:

FRESH WATER DRAINS
(Note: While draining, remove filler cap from top of expansion tank).
4 Cylinder models:
  Engine Block - Left side, front (behind alternator)
  Heat Exchanger - Underneath, right side
  Exhaust Manifold - Leftside, rear
6 Cylinder models:
  Engine Block - Left side, low (near center)
  Heat Exchange - Underneath, left side (nearest center of engine)
  Exhaust Manifold - Left side, rear

RAW WATER DRAINS
Water pump: Loosen rear cover
Lube oil cooler: Under, rear
Transmission oil cooler: under, left side
Heat exchanger: Under, left side (Note: 4 cylinder models have combination drain plug & zinc pencil)

(Note: Manual type transmissions (Lehman Series 144 or Paragon G-33 having

## "KEEL COOLING" SYSTEMS

In some cases the installation of a "keel cooling" system may be preferred to the standard "heat exchanger" previously discussed. This system employs a series of tubes mounted on the underside of the hull through which the engine cooling water is circulated. Such a system is beneficial when the boat is to operate in muddy or silt-laden areas, however, the cooling element does produce additional hull "drag" which could affect performance in faster boats and creates a potential hazard if tubes fracture or are struck by driftwood, etc.

Piping engine to keel cooler is quite simple. As shown in Fig. 14-A the connection on underside (starboard) of expansion tank delivers hot water from engine to keel cooler. Cooled water from keel cooler returns to engine via connection on aft end of exhaust manifold. The use of 1⅜" I.D. hose will simplify connections, however hose must be reinforced type to prevent collapsing under suction and care must be exercised when installing to avoid "kinks" or the possibility of chafing.

Installations using a "wet" exhaust will require raw water system as shown in Fig. 14, but omitting heat exchanger.

When dry exhaust is employed, it is possible to eliminate use of the raw water pump. Upon special order, lube and transmission oil coolers of large size may be incorporated in the engine fresh water system. The addition of such coolers is shown in Fig. 14-B.

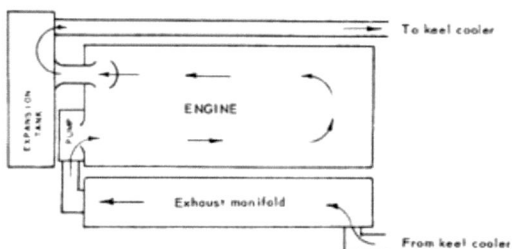

FIG. 14-A  FRESH WATER CIRCULATION SYSTEM
(Keel Cooler Type)

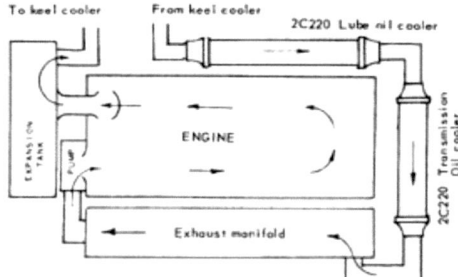

FIG. 14-B  WATER CIRCULATION SYSTEM (Keel Cooler Type)
WITH LUBE and TRANSMISSION OIL COOLERS IN
FRESH WATER FLOW.

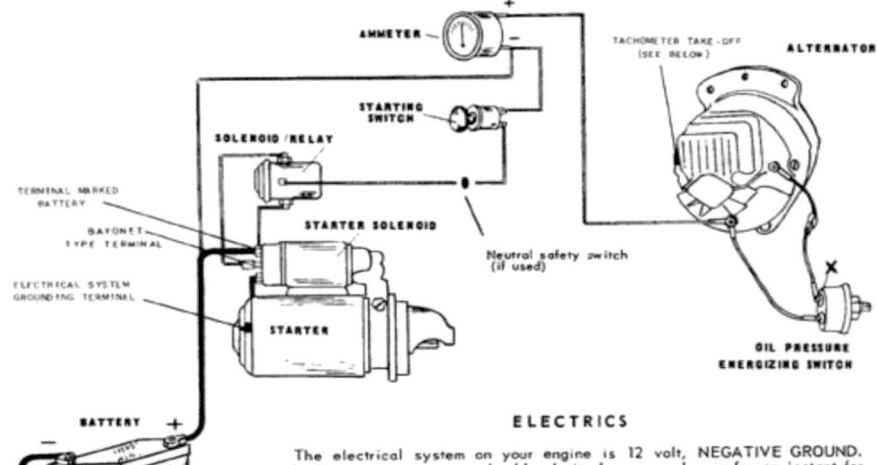

**FIG. 15**
**WIRING DIAGRAM**

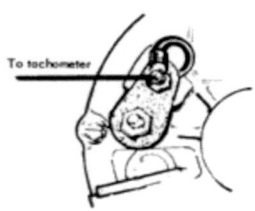

**FIG. 16**

Tap at rear of alternator for (optional) electrical tachometer.

## ELECTRICS

The electrical system on your engine is 12 volt, NEGATIVE GROUND. Under no circumstances should polarity be reversed even for an instant for serious damage to alternator may result.

A vee belt drives the alternator from crankshaft pulley. (Note: Maintain belt at proper tension - see "minor Repairs, Maintenance and Adjustments"). Alternator has been corrosion-treated and has built-in silicon rectifier and enclosed slip-ring design for safe, sparkless, trouble-free operation. Transistor type, sealed voltage regulator is built into the alternator making one compact unit. The regulator has no moving parts and requires no adjustments. Alternator is lubricant packed for life at time of assembly and therefore requires no external lubrication. Starting Sept. 1972 alternators (designated model 8MR2018-K) are equipped with a tapping (see fig. 16) for connection to operate a matching electric tachometer (optional).

A special actuating switch located on side of engine block behind alternator automatically energizes the alternator from the battery when engine is started and oil pressure reaches 7 lbs. Battery is disconnected by this switch when the engine is stopped. This switch initiates operation of the alternator system without the need of a separate switch and precludes the possibility of the operator neglecting to turn the charging system on or off. If desired, electrical instruments such as oil gage, temperature gage, etc. may be wired to be automatically energized when engine is started.

The starter motor is located on the left side (rear) of engine and requires no attention beyond maintaining the electric cable connections clean and tight, the commutator clean and brushes renewed when neccessary.

The standard solenoid mounted on the starting motor is a heavy-duty type. It must mechanically engage the starter pinion with the ring gear on flywheel; then it must actuate an electric switch to energize the starting motor. As the solenoid is normally energized by a simple push-button located at some distance from the starter, relatively heavy gage wire is required to transmit the needed amperage. Using small gage wire can result in insufficient current reaching the starter solenoid, overheating of wires, insufficient travel of starter pinion and failure of engine to start.

To assure adaquate amperage reaching starter solenoid a "piggy-back" solenoid is provided with short, heavy-gage wires connecting the two solenoids. The new solenoid requires comparitively little amperage so smaller gage wiring is required for connection to pushbutton.

The accompanying diagram indicates basic wiring requirements. Make certain that all connections are clean and tight. Locate battery as close as practical to the starter. Gage of battery cables will be dependent upon length, but should be NO. 0 minimum. Use No. 12 gage or heavier wire for balance of system. Electrical gages which require low current draw may be wired to oil pressure energizing switch indicated by "X" on the diagram.

## TACHOMETER ADAPTER

A tachometer "take-off" is provided on the starboard side of your engine near center of engine block. This adapter accommodates a standard marine tachometer cable with 7/8" - 18 adaptor nut. Tip of cable core should be .187" diameter. Cable turns one-half engine speed in counter-clockwise direction.

If mechanical tachometer is not used or if cable is disconnected with engine to be operated for any lengthy period, the take-off should be capped to prevent oil leakage. Suitable cap (or plug to close aperature if take-off assembly is removed) is listed in the parts section of this manual.

It is recommended that a mechanical type tachometer be used only if located relatively close to engine. If cable length exceeds 12 to 14 feet or if many bends are required, an electrical tachometer system should be considered as much less strain is placed upon the take-off assembly. Installations requiring two tachometers should always use electric instruments.

## LUBRICATION SYSTEM

The engine lubricating system is of the forced feed type, the oil being circulated by an oil pump mounted within the crankcase. The pump draws oil from the sump through a metal gauze screen and through an oil gallery on the port (left) side of engine which is tapped for installation of oil pressure gauge, low oil pressure alarm, or other such devices. Constant oil pressure is maintained by means of a relief valve situated in the pump. Oil under pressure passes through the oil filter where it is cleaned prior to being circulated inside the engine. The filter is a full-flow, disposable "spin-on" type of automotive design and easily available through automotive suppliers. It should be replaced at each oil change.

All marine installations should include an oil pressure gauge to register the lube system pressure and such gauge should be frequently checked to insure that system is functioning correctly. Normally the registered pressure should remain constant for a given engine speed. If pressure reading suddenly varies or fluctuates, the reason should be determined at once, otherwise severe damage may occur. As it is difficult to maintain a constant watch on engine gauges, the use of an audible warning system to sound a buzzer in case of low oil pressure (or high engine temperature) is strongly recommended.

The oil sump capacity of various model engine is shown under "Specifications". But note that such capacities are calculated when engine is level. As your engine will probably be installed at an angle, the dipstick provided for measuring oil level in the crankcase must be remarked. (Note that the dipstick on your engine may be installed on either the port or starboard side).

When engine is first installed, provide the proper quantity of oil as indicated under "specifications" section. The oil fill cap is located on top of engine rocker arm cover. After pouring in oil, it will be necessary to wait several minutes before the oil level is checked in order to allow time for oil to flow to sump. Another fill cap which leads directly to sump is located on sump near front of engine. Run engine for several moments, shut down and check level on dipstick (see figure 17). If oil level measurement is different from the "full" mark on dipstick, a new mark should be scratched or filed at the correct level. When measuring oil level in regular usage it is preferable to check after the engine has stopped for a period of time, such as overnight. This allows the oil in the overhead valve system to drain back to the oil sump, permitting a more accurate measurement. Add engine oil of the type and viscosity recommended as follows:

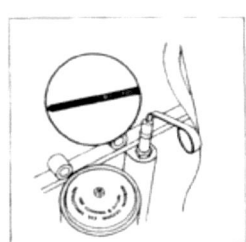

FIG. 17
ENGINE OIL DIPSTICK

**IMPORTANT**
LUBE OIL CLEANLINESS IS VITAL FOR THE LONG LIFE OF YOUR ENGINE. WHEN CHANGING OR ADDING OIL, USE CLEAN RECEPTICLES.

| ENGINE OIL RECOMMENDATIONS ||
|---|---|
| NATURALLY ASPIRATED MODELS: | API CLASSIFICATION CC |
| TURBOCHARGED MODELS: | API CLASSIFICATION CD or SERIES III |
| Average Temp. (F) | SAE Viscosity |
| -10° to 32° | 10W |
| 10° to 60° | 20W |
| 32° to 90° | 30 |
| Over 90° | 40 |

## LUBRICATION SYSTEM (Continued)

TURBO ENGINES: API classification CD oils only must be used in turbocharged engines. Use of other oil will result in reduced engine life and will invalidate engine warranty.

Serious damage to turbocharger may result from inadequate lubrication. Upon starting, engine should be allowed to idle (1000 rpm maximum) for 30 seconds or more before applying load. Also allow engine to idle for at least one minute before shut-down to dissipate heat from turbocharger bearings.

Turbocharger must be oil-primed under any one of following conditions:
- After an oil change.
- If oil supply tube to turbocharger has been disconnected.
- If either the engine or turbocharger is newly installed.
- If no oil pressure registers on gage after a "dead crank" (cranking with stop control in operation) for 10 seconds. This test must be performed if engine has not been started for 4 weeks or more.

To oil-prime turbocharger:
a) Check for sufficient oil in the engine sump but do not top-up at this time.
b) Disconnect the oil feed tube at the turbocharger end and fill the housing with oil. Reconnect tube.
c) Using suitable syringe, inject about 4 pints of oil (as used in engine sump) into oil gage connection of engine. Refit oil gage.
d) Start engine, allowing 1 minute to idle before increasing speed.
e) Stop engine and check sump oil level. Top-off if needed or drain off any surplus.

Engine oil should be changed after the initial 15 hours of operation and at each 200 hours of operation thereafter. Run the engine until normal operating temperature is reached. Shut down engine and allow oil to return to sump for five to ten minutes. In most installations it will not be possible to drain sump by removing plug which is located at bottom of oil pan, for clearance to bilge of hull will be limited. A low-cost, suction type, hand operated sump pump is required. Remove the dip-stick tube and insert suction hose of pump, working same towards lower portion of sump. (Some operators find it advantageous to use a length of copper tubing to assure reaching low section of sump.) Pump oil into container and dispose of same ashore. Replace vent cap on sump. Refill crankcase to "full" mark on dipstick. Run engine for several minutes, shut down and recheck oil level. If required, add sufficient oil to bring up to full mark.

Lube oil filter element should be replaced at each oil change. The disposable element is simply unscrewed from its base by turning counter-clockwise. Position a one-quart or larger container under filter before removal to catch oil from spilling into bilge. A new element is simply screwed onto the base with medium hand tightness. Under no circumstances should a wrench or excess pressure be used. When next starting engine, check filter for possible leaks or seepage, and tighten only sufficiently to prevent same.

The sump of the Simms fuel injection pump carries a supply of oil to lubricate the intricate mechanism contained within the housing. It is imperative that this unit be properly and regularly serviced. (See fig. 18)

Oil level must be checked when engine is first placed in service, before initial start-up and at intervals as specified in the Maintenance section. Oil should be changed after initial 15 engine hours operation, and at 50-hour intervals thereafter. Drain the sump oil by removing drain plug located on bottom of housing. Replace drain plug and remove filler plug from top of injection pump and oil level plug located at side of housing, above drain plug. Add engine oil (same type and viscosity as used in engine sump) through the filler orifice until oil reaches the level plug opening. Do not overfill as this may cause improper operation and cause excess oil to leak out of injection pump. Replace oil level and filler plugs.

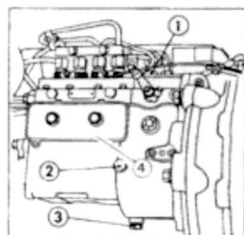

FIG. 18
INJECTION PUMP

1 - Filling plug
2 - Oil level plug
3 - Drain plug
4 - Side cover

## TRANSMISSION

As there is such a wide variety of transmissions available with Lehman diesels, it is not practical to cover all installations in this manual. However, due to the popularity of Paragon and Warner transmissions, the following information is offered for these models.

No attempt is made herein to instruct in the installation of engine in the boat. The prudent boat owner or operator will, before initially starting engine, check engine/shaft alignment, operate clutch control to make certain that lever fully travels to the full ahead or full reverse positions, that neutral position may easily and quickly be found, and, of course, check oil level.

The transmission is a self-contained, sealed unit with independent lubrication system. No external adjustments of any kind are required. A built-in oil pump supplies the required hydraulic pressure to provide effortless shifting and assures an adequate supply of lubricant to all moving parts. An oil cooler is provided in order to maintain proper oil temperature which should not exceed 190°F.

Automatic transmission fluid type A, suffix A is recommended for lubrication. Or, if desired, "Dexron" type fluid may be used. Before starting engine fill transmission to the full mark on the dipstick. Run engine for a minute or two at low speed (in order to fill oil lines, cooler, etc.) then shut off engine and check oil level. Add sufficient oil to bring up to full mark. Transmission oil level should be checked each time the oil level in engine is checked. Change oil every 200 hours of operation or at least once each season under normal conditions, however, number of hours may vary depending upon severity and conditions of service. WARNER drain plug is a large "hex" plug located near bottom right side. To drain, remove plug and pull out strainer. (fig. 19). PARAGON drain plugs are located at bottom of reverse gear housing and reduction gear housing. (fig. 20)

A low-cost "sump pump" provides easy method of changing oil without removal of drain plugs.

PARAGON transmissions are normally provided with offset DOWN (propeller shaft flange BELOW the engine crankshaft). To revolve offset to UP position, disassemble reduction gear case from transmission by removing the 6 or 8 capscrews. Be careful not to damage gasket. You will now be able to remove the 6 or 8 socket-head cap screws which hold the reduction adaptor plate to transmission case. This adaptor can be revolved to desired position. (Note It may be necessary to tap the adaptor with a mallet or hardwood block in order to break its "set" to the transmission case). Make certain to replace any damaged gaskets. (Note: Paragon transmissions which reverse propeller shaft rotation - Lehman models D155BP and D156BP - cannot have offset revolved to the "up" position).

WARNING: Once again we repeat - control cable or other mechanism for shifting transmission must have sufficient "throw" to shift the operating lever fully into both forward or reverse position. Unless shift lever is positively in forward, neutral or reverse, considerable damage may result. Transmission warranty is void if control lever is changed in any manner, or repositioned or if linkage to remote control does not have sufficient travel in both directions.

When ordering parts for your transmission be sure to specify both model and serial numbers as shown on identification tag.

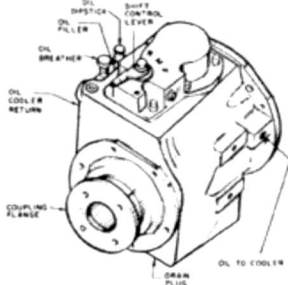

FIG. 20
PARAGON TRANSMISSION

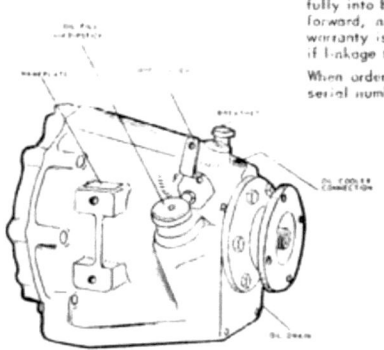

FIG. 19
WARNER TRANSMISSION

## MAINTENANCE

The importance of correct lubrication, periodic inspection and adjustment cannot be over-emphasised. On it will depend, to a very large extent, the service which your engine will deliver.

The heat exchanger of your engine is protected by a "zinc pencil" which should be inspected and replaced periodically, as required. As the rate of electrolysis varies greatly in different areas, only experience will dictate how often inspections should be made.

For convenience, lubrication and maintenance work has been divided into the following periods:

(a) After first 15 hours running.
(b) After every 10 hours running.
(c) After every 50 hours running.
(d) After every 200 hours running.
(e) After every 400 hours running.

### SUMMARY OF REGULAR MAINTENANCE

After first 15 hours running . . . . 
1. Change Engine Oil
2. Tighten cylinder head retaining bolts.
3. Adjust valve clearances.
4. Check (exchanger) zinc pencil.
5. Adjust belt tension.
6. Check injection pump oil level.
7. Check transmission oil level.
8. Check cleanliness of intake air filter.
9. Check engine/propeller shaft alignment. (twice annually, minimum).
10. Adjust idling speed (if required).

Every 10 hours running . . . . . . 
11. Check engine and transmission oil levels.
12. Check cooling water level.

Every 50 hours running . . . . . . 
13. Check cleanliness of intake air filter.
14. Check (exchanger) zinc pencil.
15. Change oil in injection pump.

Every 200 hours running . . . . . 
16. Adjust belt tension.
17. Change engine and transmission oil.
18. Change all engine and fuel oil filters.
19. Clean fuel lift pump.
20. Clean injection pump cover filter.

Every 400 hours running . . . . . 
21. Remove and service injectors.
22. Adjust valve clearances.
23. Remove raw water pump and check drive coupling. Place dab of grease on coupling halves when replacing.
24. Adjust idling speed (if required).
25. Check torque of cylinder head bolts (turbo only).

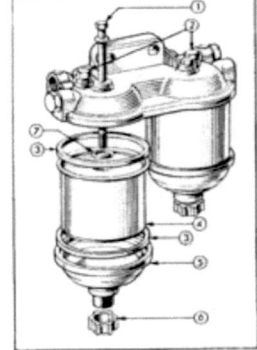

FIG. 21
FUEL FILTER
1 - Securing bolt
2 - Bleed screws
3 - Sealing rings
4 - Filter element
5 - Bowl
6 - Drain cap
7 - Sealing ring

To change fuel filter element: (note- make certain that the filter element(s) you will use is an EXACT replacement for the element you will remove, otherwise, air leaks into the fuel system may result). Unscrew the securing bolts on top of filter housing (see fig. 21) and remove filter bowls and elements. Discard elements and upper and lower sealing rings. Wash out the bowls and clean fuel oil but do not use a cloth for remaining lint may clog the fuel system. Carefully fit new sealing rings to the filter heads and bowls, assemble to the filter heads and replace and tighten securing bolts. It will now be necessary to bleed the fuel system of air as described in separate section. After running engine for a short time, check filters for possible fuel leaks.

## MINOR REPAIRS, MAINTENANCE & ADJUSTMENTS

TO TIGHTEN CYLINDER HEAD BOLTS: Start and run engine until normal operating temperature is reached. Stop engine. Remove rocker arm cover from top of engine. Tighten cylinder head bolts in sequence as shown in figures 22 and 23 to a torque of 105 to 110 ft/lbs., engine hot. (130-135 ft/lbs. for turbo models). Check valve clearances before replacing rocker arm cover.

NOTE: A NEW GASKET SHOULD BE AVAILABLE BEFORE REMOVING THE ROCKER ARM COVER IN CASE OF DAMAGE TO THE ONE PRESENTLY IN USE.

FIG. 22 - BOLT TIGHTENING SEQUENCE (4 Cyl.)

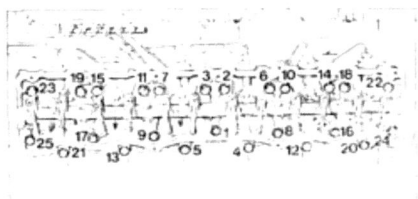

FIG. 23 - BOLT TIGHTENING SEQUENCE (6 Cyl.)

TO ADJUST VALVE CLEARANCES: (Note . . Adjustments should be made while engine is at normal operating temperature). Following removal of rocker arm cover and tightening cylinder head bolts as described above, actuate the engine stop control lever so engine will not start and revolve crankshaft (Note: 4 cylinder models are fitted with a barring plate at crankshaft pulley, figure 24) until numbers 1 and 6 valves (on 4 cylinder) or numbers 1 and 4 (on 6 cylinder) are opened by their respective rocker arms.

Insert the correct thickness feeler gage (as shown in the following table) between the valve stem cap and rocker arm of No. 3 inlet valve (on 4 cylinder) or No. 9 inlet valve (on 6 cylinder) as shown in figure 25. Turn the valve clearance adjusting screw until the feeler blade is lightly caught between the rocker arm and valve stem cap, but so that the blade can still be removed with light resistance.

Select the appropriate feeler blade and repeat the procedure for No. 8 exhaust valve (on 4 cylinder) or No. 12 exhaust valve (on 6 cylinder models).

Rotate the engine and, following the sequence in following table, adjust each of the remaining valves. Replace rocker cover, making certain that gasket is unbroken and correctly positioned. After running engine for a short while, check rocker arm cover gasket for possible oil leaks.

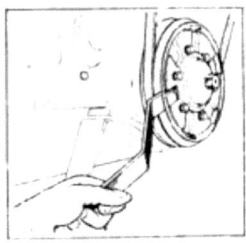

FIG. 24
ENGINE BARRING PLATE
(4 Cyl. only)

### VALVE CLEARANCES (Engine at normal working temperature)

|  | INLET | EXHAUST |
|---|---|---|
| NORMALLY ASPIRATED | .015" | .012" |
| TURBO-CHARGED | .018" | .018" |

### ADJUSTMENT SEQUENCE - 4 CYL. MODELS
(Valves are numbered starting at front of engine)

| Valves Open | Valves To Adjust |
|---|---|
| 1 and 6 | 3 In. and 8 Ex. |
| 2 and 4 | 5 Ex. and 7 In. |
| 3 and 8 | 1 Ex. and 6 In. |
| 5 and 7 | 2 In. and 4 Ex. |

### ADJUSTMENT SEQUENCE - 6 CYL. MODELS

| Valves Open | Valves To Adjust |
|---|---|
| 1 and 4 | 9 In. and 12 Ex. |
| 8 and 10 | 3 Ex. and 5 In. |
| 2 and 6 | 7 Ex. and 11 In. |
| 9 and 12 | 1 Ex. and 4 In. |
| 3 and 5 | 8 In. and 10 Ex. |
| 7 and 11 | 2 In. and 6 Ex. |

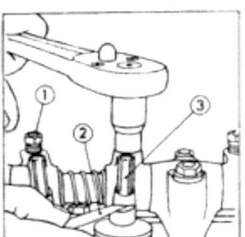

FIG. 25
ADJUSTING VALVE CLEARANCE
1- Adjusting screw
2- Feeler blade
3- Rocker arm

## MINOR REPAIRS, MAINTENANCE & ADJUSTMENTS (Continued)

**TO ADJUST VEE BELT TENSION:** Loosen alternator mounting and adjusting strap bolts as per figure 26. Move alternator to adjust belt tension. Tension is correct when your thumb pressure on belt at a point between alternator and water pump pulleys does not exceed 1/4". Tighten alternator mounting and adjustment strap bolts.

**INTAKE AIR FILTER:** The air filtering element(s) on your engine is polyurethan foam which traps and holds dust and foreign matter which could be drawn into the engine and cause severe damage. DO NOT OPERATE ENGINE WITHOUT HAVING FILTER IN PLACE.

By reason of the efficiency of the filter in trapping contaminants it is difficult to effectively clean the element. It is usually best to replace this low-cost item as occasion demands. Simply slide old element off its retaining screen and carefully stretch a new element into position. If cleaning is desired, wash in a mild detergent mixed in clear, sweet water. DO NOT wash in mineral spirits, varsol, gasoline, or any petroleum product.

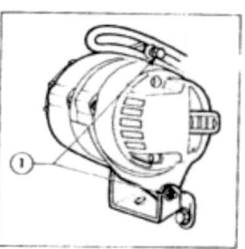

FIG. 26
BELT ADJUSTMENT
1 - Adjusting bolts

**TO ADJUST IDLING SPEED:** When properly serviced and after the initial "break-in" period, your engine should idle within a general range of 600 to 700 RPM; when new, idle speed may be somewhat higher.

Engine must be at normal operating temperature when making adjustments. With engine running, loosen the idle stop locknut (figure 27) which is on side of fuel injection pump (between pump and engine block). Adjust the idle speed screw until engine is idling at correct speed and then tighten locknut. Operate the throttle lever to make certain that same returns to same setting.

To adjust for "surging" or erratic idle, carefully adjust the "damper" screw (figure 27) at rear of injection pump. Turn the damper screw in (clockwise) until engine idle speed just starts to increase, then loosen damper screw (turning counter-clockwise) SLIGHTLY. The adjustment at this point is quite critical and should be made by adjusting the screw 1/8 turn at a time, increasing the throttle momentarily between each trial setting until the most favorable adjustment is obtained. Turning the damper screw IN too far will increase the engine idle speed and require resetting the idle stop screw.

Note: If engine is new or cold, it may idle unevenly. Do not increase the idle speed setting to compensate. ON NO ACCOUNT SHOULD THE MAXIMUM SPEED STOP BE CHANGED.

**TO REMOVE INJECTORS:** Remove the rocker arm cover from top of engine. Remove the fuel leak-off pipe (fig. 28) by unscrewing the union nut at rear of cylinder head and the bolts connecting leak-off pipe to each injector. Care must be exercised not to bend or damage fuel injector pipes so it is suggested that the union nuts at top of injection pump (fig. 29) be loosened after first removing the injector pipe clamp(s).

Slacken each of the oil seal nuts (fig. 28) on side of cylinder head and by unscrewing the fuel inlet adaptor nuts, remove adaptors from the injectors.

Unscrew the two bolts securing each injector to the cylinder head and carefully remove injectors, making certain that no foreign matter drops into the cavity. A low cost "injector removing tool" will assist in this operation (fig. 30). Remove the copper sealing washer from the injector housing if same is not removed with the injector. New sealing washers should be used when replacing. Note: Special equipment is required for servicing injector, and this should not be attempted by the novice.

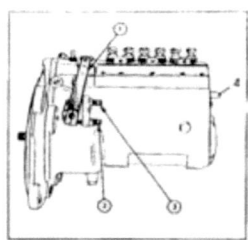

FIG. 27
INJECTION PUMP
1 - Speed control lever
2 - Max. speed stop screw
3 - Idling stop screw
4 - Idle damper screw

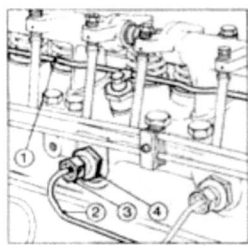

FIG. 28
INJECTOR PIPES
1 - Fuel leak-off pipe
2 - Injector pipe
3 - Inlet adaptor nut
4 - Oil seal nut

**TO CLEAN FUEL LIFT PUMP:** Turn off fuel supply valve. Holding receptacle under pump to prevent spilling of fuel into bilge of boat, loosen the center bolt (fig. 31) and remove cover and pulsator. Clean pump thoroughly and wash cover and pulsator in fuel oil. Replace parts carefully. It will be necessary to bleed fuel system. Check for possible leaks after starting engine.

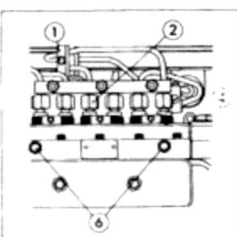

FIG. 29
INJECTION PUMP
1 - Injector pipe clamp
2 - Union nut
6 - Bleed screws

FIG. 30
INJECTOR REMOVING TOOL

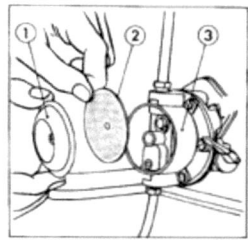

FIG. 31
FUEL LIFT PUMP
(Except turbo)
1 - Cover
2 - Diaphragm
3 - Pump body

## WINTERIZING

In preparation for freezing temperatures, anti-freeze should be provided in the fresh water system of your engine. Due to the high temperature of operation, a high boiling point anti-freeze is demanded. Do not attempt to use alcohol or other non-permanent types and do not use any liquids containing "sealants". Zerex (produced by DuPont) is highly recommended. Consult the specification chart of your engine to determine its coolant capacity and add sufficient anti-freeze to bring within the limits of expected temperatures.

Inboard type heat exchangers and oil coolers must be drained of raw (sea) water when exposed to freezing temperatures. Drain plugs will be found on bottom of heat exchanger and oil coolers and should be removed until all water has been drained. Raw water pump may be drained by loosening screws holding rear cover in position.

If boat is to remain in water while draining engine, of course, the intake water seacock must be closed prior to draining. Do not neglect to open seacock prior to starting engine.

NOTE: TO DRAIN FRESH WATER, REMOVE WATER FILLER CAP FROM TOP OF EXPANSION TANK ON FRONT OF ENGINE. DRAIN BLOCK BY OPENING PETCOCK ON PORT (LEFT) SIDE OF ENGINE IN CENTER, LOWER SECTION. REMOVE PLUG ON UNDERSIDE OF HEAT EXCHANGER (THE ONE NEAREST CENTER OF EXCHANGER) TO DRAIN WATER FROM EXCHANGER, EXPANSION TANK AND EXHAUST MANIFOLD. REPLACE FILL CAP ON TANK AFTER ALL WATER HAS DRAINED.

Remove air filter(s) and cover openings in manifold with plastic film held in place with masking tape. Seal off all other openings . . . air vent on top of rocker arm cover, vent on front end of sump and overflow and vent hole or injection pump. Plug exhaust pipe to prevent entrance of moisture.

Make certain that all engine exterior surfaces are clean, dry and free of oil or grease; then spray complete engine with any good rust preventative compound.

Before restarting engine, remove all plastic seals, covers, exhaust plug, etc., and refit air filter(s) in place. Do not neglect to replace all drain plugs, tighten rear cover of raw water pump, and turn on seacock.

## HOT WATER HEATER CONNECTIONS

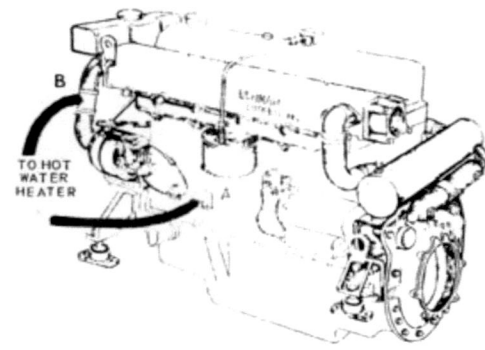

It is common marine practice to use heat produced by the engine for on-board hot water requirements. A portion of the (fresh water) engine coolant is directed through a "galley hot water heater" which provides the required heat transfer.

Connection to engine (for supplying hot engine coolant to the water heater) is made from engine block drain fitting located at lower, center of block on port side. See "A" in accompanying sketch. A tee fitting will allow this connection, while retaining the convenient drain cock.

Coolant return to engine is made into the formed front water hose leading to the fresh water pump. See "B" in sketch.

Lehman offers a complete "Galley hot water heater connection kit" as optional equipment.

## BOLT TIGHTENING TORQUE LIMITS (ft. lbs.)

| Fastener | Torque | Fastener | Torque |
|---|---|---|---|
| Oil Pan Drain Plug | 30-40 | Injector Retaining Bolts | 12-15 |
| Oil Pump to Cylinder Block | 12-15 | Injector Inlet Adaptor to injector | 16-20 |
| Oil Pump Cover Plate | 12-15 | Injector Oil Seal Locknut | 16-20 |
| Oil Pick-up Tube to Oil Pump | 12-15 | Injector Pipe Nut (pump end) | 16-20 |
| Oil Pan to Cylinder Block | 22-24 | Injection Pump Bleed Screws | 3-5 |
| Main Bearing Cap bolts | 115-120 | Leak-off Pipe to Injector Bolt | 12-15 |
| Connecting Rod bolts | 85-90 | Leak-off Pipe Banjo Connector | 12-15 |
| Cylinder Head Bolts (engine hot) | 105-110 | Injection Pump Retaining bolts | 22-27 |
| Cylinder Head Bolts (turbo only) | 130-145 | Injection Pump Fill, Level & Drain Plugs | 3-5 |
| Crankshaft center bolt | 240 | Valve rocker Cover Bolts | 12-18 |
| Engine Mounting bolts | 35-40 | Fuel (lift) Pump Center Bolt | 7-10 |
| Rocker Shaft Bracket bolts | 17-22 | Fuel Filter Bracket bolts | 12-15 |
| Front Housing to Cylinder Block | 25-30 | Fuel Filter Bleed Screws | 5-7 |
| Camshaft Thrust Plate | 25-30 | Fuel (lift) Pump Mounting bolts | 12-15 |
| Exhaust Manifold Retaining bolts | 20-25 | Alternator Support Bracket bolts | 12-15 |
| Exhaust Manifold Outlet Flange | 22-27 | Alternator Adjusting Strap bolt | 12-15 |
| Expansion (water) Tank Nuts | 12-15 | | |
| Flywheel to Crankshaft flange bolts | 80-90 | | |

Torque limits for various size bolts except as listed above:

| Size | Torque |
|---|---|
| 1/4" diameter | 6-9 |
| 5/16-18 | 12-15 |
| 5/16-24 | 15-18 |
| 3/8-16 | 23-28 |
| 3/8-24 | 30-35 |
| 7/16-14 | 45-50 |
| 7/16-20 | 50-60 |
| 1/2-13 | 60-70 |
| 1/2-20 | 70-80 |
| 9/16-18 | 85-95 |
| 5/8-18 | 130-145 |